Original title:
The Geometry of Genuine Gestures

Copyright © 2024 Swan Charm
All rights reserved.

Author: Kaido Väinamäe
ISBN HARDBACK: 978-9916-86-626-9
ISBN PAPERBACK: 978-9916-86-627-6
ISBN EBOOK: 978-9916-86-628-3

Nexus of Nurturance

In the garden of the heart, we sow,
Tender seeds of kindness, they grow.
Sunlight streams, as hope takes flight,
A gentle whisper in the night.

Roots entwined in sacred trust,
We rise together, as we must.
In the soil where love is laid,
Blooming dreams shall never fade.

Through storms that shake, and winds that wail,
We stand as one, we shall not frail.
With hands held tight, we brave the fight,
In unity, we find our light.

Each moment shared, a precious thread,
Woven tight, where fears are shed.
In laughter's echo, peace takes hold,
A tapestry of love unfolds.

Beneath the stars, our voices blend,
A symphony that knows no end.
In this nexus where spirits thrive,
Together, we shall always strive.

Angles of Affection

In the light of a gentle dawn,
Hearts find warmth where love is drawn.
Each glance a brush, each touch a hue,
Painting life in colors true.

Whispers soft like the evening breeze,
Holding moments, simple, with ease.
In every laugh, a spark ignites,
Guiding souls to shared delights.

Through shadows long and pathways wide,
Kindness lingers, it won't hide.
Angles shift, but love remains,
Binding hearts with unseen chains.

In the eyes where secrets dwell,
Echoes of stories we dare tell.
A tapestry woven, day by day,
In angles of affection, we find our way.

Proportions of Peace

In quiet corners, peace takes root,
With every pulse, a gentle flute.
Harmony sings, soft and low,
Filling hearts with a healing flow.

The sun dips down, the world stands still,
Nature's canvas, a sacred thrill.
In every sigh, serenity glows,
A melody where stillness grows.

Bridges built on kindness shared,
In the silence, love declared.
Amidst the noise, a quiet grace,
In the proportions, we find our place.

As oceans ebb and tides recede,
Soft whispers plant the hopeful seed.
With each heartbeat, we learn to see,
The beautiful dance of harmony.

Blueprint of Belonging

Lines drawn light beneath the stars,
Where shadows fade, and laughter jars.
In every space, a story grows,
A map of love, as the heart knows.

Found in moments, small and bright,
Connections forged in silent light.
In shared glances, the truth unfolds,
In blueprints made with hearts of gold.

Voices blend like a perfect tune,
Under the watch of the silver moon.
In every smile, a place to land,
An embrace, a gentle hand.

Through winding paths, together we roam,
Crafting a world that feels like home.
In the blueprint of belonging's claim,
Forever marked, we'll stake our name.

Tapestry of Tenderness

Threads of care in every weave,
Intertwined, we dare believe.
With gentle hands, we craft the art,
A tapestry where we play a part.

Colorful fibers spanning wide,
In every hue, a story bides.
Softness found in heart's embrace,
Creating warmth, a sacred space.

With whispered hopes and dreams unfurled,
We stitch together our shared world.
In every tear, we weave the light,
Resilience shines throughout the night.

Each moment passed, a thread we save,
In the tender ties, we find the brave.
Tapestry rich, forever strong,
Together, we belong where we belong.

The Blueprint of Belonging

In quiet corners, hearts align,
A map of dreams, a shared design.
We gather voices, threads entwined,
In every heartbeat, love defined.

Branches of laughter, roots of pain,
Together through sun and through rain.
Each story whispers, each hand held,
In unity's strength, we are impelled.

With every step, we navigate,
The paths we choose, the friends we make.
Through trials faced and joys we share,
A tapestry of hope laid bare.

Harmony builds, a sacred space,
Infinite kindness, a warm embrace.
No place like this, where we belong,
In the symphony of love's great song.

Spirals of Sincere Care

In gentle whispers, love begins,
Encircling hearts, where trust shall spin.
Acts of kindness, like rivers flow,
In every hand that helps, we grow.

Through winding paths, together we tread,
With open hearts, and words unsaid.
Caring glances, a tender grace,
In each moment, we find our place.

The spiral deepens, layers unfold,
A dance of spirits, both brave and bold.
We lean on each other, through joy and strife,
In the heart's embrace, we find our life.

Each circular turn brings us near,
With every cycle, we persevere.
In the web of compassion, we are bound,
A sanctuary of solace found.

The Axis of Authenticity

At the center lies our truest core,
Where voices rise and spirits soar.
With every truth, we chip away,
The masks we wear, in light of day.

Real words spoken, in love's embrace,
We share our stories, each face a grace.
In openness, we craft our bonds,
In honest moments, a world responds.

The axis spins on trust and care,
As we unveil what's truly rare.
Expressing feelings, raw and real,
In the dance of life, we learn to feel.

Embrace the flaws, the scars we bear,
In our honesty, no need to compare.
Connected deeply, we navigate,
In the realm of truth, we elevate.

Tangles of Tenderness

In the softest light, our hands entwine,
Each touch a promise, a sign divine.
In tangled moments, warmth ignites,
Threads of affection weave our nights.

With laughter blooming, hearts expand,
In gentle chaos, we take a stand.
The beauty blooms in the messy parts,
Tangles of tenderness fill our hearts.

We wrap around each fragile dream,
In the quiet whispers, love will gleam.
Each challenge faced, a chance to grow,
In bonds of affections, our hearts bestow.

Through winding paths, our stories blend,
In the tapestry of life, we depend.
Embracing flaws, we find our way,
In tangles of tenderness, love will stay.

Symmetry of Softness

In twilight's calm embrace,
Whispers dance like gentle air.
Each touch a soft caress,
In harmony, we share.

Petals fall without a sound,
Mirroring the heart's true grace.
In silence, love is found,
A heartbeat's warm embrace.

Moonlight bathes the quiet night,
Casting shadows, soothing light.
In the stillness, dreams take flight,
As stars wink with pure delight.

Every sigh a symphony,
Every glance a tender note.
In the space between you and me,
An endless love I wrote.

As morning spills its golden hue,
Soft reflections, pure and bright.
Our bond, a canvas painted anew,
In the symmetry of light.

Patterns of Empathy

In the fabric of our days,
Threads of kindness weave so tight.
Every heart a subtle praise,
A tapestry of shared light.

Through the storms we stand as one,
Each struggle makes us strong and wise.
In the warmth of every sun,
Compassion leads us to the skies.

With every tear, a story told,
In every laugh, a moment shared.
In the patterns, a heart unfolds,
Together, we are truly paired.

We rise to meet each other's eyes,
Mirroring what love can be.
In our connection, no disguise,
Just pure and true empathy.

When shadows linger, we ignite,
Paths aligned in shared intent.
In the depths of darkest night,
Together, we find our ascent.

Shapes of Sincerity

In the garden, truths arise,
Petals bloom from honest ground.
With each glance, the heart complies,
In sincerity, we're found.

When words are clear, and feelings flow,
A rhythm gentle as a stream.
In trust, we let our spirits grow,
Building bridges, living dreams.

Like clouds that shift, our hearts reveal,
Shapes of honesty, pure and grand.
In vulnerability, we heal,
Holding tightly hand in hand.

In moments shared, a quiet grace,
Reflections of a steadfast will.
In each other's warm embrace,
A love that's genuine and still.

When the night wraps us in peace,
And whispers of the true remain,
In sincerity, we find release,
In love's embrace, we break the chain.

Vectors of Valor

In the face of stormy skies,
Courage rises with the dawn.
With every step, our spirits fly,
In valor's light, we are drawn.

Through fire and fear, we strive to stand,
Each heartbeat a resolute beat.
In unity, we take command,
Brothers, sisters, strong on our feet.

With every challenge that we meet,
We carve our paths, fierce and clear.
In the shadows, we won't retreat,
For in togetherness, we steer.

Across horizons blazing bright,
Our hopes unfurl like banners high.
In the journey, we find our might,
The stars will guide, we'll reach the sky.

In the echoes of our fight,
The spirit of bravery blooms.
For in each heart, a guiding light,
A legacy that always looms.

Radiance in Reciprocity

In the warmth of shared smiles,
We find our glowing light,
Every hand given freely,
Turn shadows into bright.

Together we bloom, not alone,
A garden of heart's grace,
With kindness as our foundation,
A sacred, joyful space.

Through laughter and gentle words,
We weave connections tight,
In the tapestry of friendship,
Our spirits take flight.

Each gesture shines like starlight,
Reflecting love's embrace,
A dance of mutual giving,
In this boundless place.

We rise, stronger united,
In harmony we thrive,
Radiance in reciprocity,
Together we feel alive.

Spaces of Support

In quiet corners shared,
We build with open hearts,
Where every voice is valued,
And each journey starts.

A gentle nod, a soft glance,
In silence we convey,
The strength found in our presence,
In every single day.

Through storms and sunny skies,
Our faith in each other shines,
Creating spaces of comfort,
Where every spirit climbs.

A refuge for the weary,
With arms both wide and free,
In spaces of support,
We simply let it be.

Together we are stronger,
Each challenge faced as one,
In unity we blossom,
Like flowers in the sun.

Dots of Delight

In the laughter of a child,
Joy dances on the air,
Every smile a small dot,
A moment's spark to share.

In the colors of the sunset,
We find a soothing sight,
Each hue a dot of delight,
Painting day into night.

A compliment, a small gift,
A gesture, soft and bright,
Each act a dot of kindness,
Adding joy to our plight.

In the rhythm of our steps,
In songs that hearts ignite,
We can gather these moments,
As dots of pure delight.

Together let us cherish,
Each spark we find in life,
Creating a constellation,
Amidst the daily strife.

Fractals of Forgiveness

In the labyrinth of our hearts,
Mistakes can intertwine,
Yet the beauty of forgiveness,
Is a fractal, divine.

With every tear we shed,
A pattern to unfold,
Healing through understanding,
As stories are retold.

Like branches of a tree,
We grow from pain to light,
Fractals of forgiveness,
Bringing the dark to bright.

In the echoes of our past,
Lessons softly play,
Each spiral brings us closer,
To love's guiding way.

In the end, we discover,
The grace in letting go,
Forgiveness, a sweet fractal,
That helps our hearts to grow.

Angles of Kindness

In hidden corners, gentle rays,
Small acts of love, in myriad ways.
A smile, a nod, a helping hand,
In every heart, these angles stand.

A bridge of warmth, where shadows flee,
Binding souls in harmony.
With whispered words, in silent night,
Kindness blooms, a pure delight.

Each gesture soft, a tender start,
Transforming worlds, a work of art.
In every eye, a spark ignites,
Guiding us through the darkest nights.

With open arms, we intertwine,
In kindness shared, our spirits shine.
Together we weave a tapestry,
Of love and grace, a symphony.

Let angles meet in open space,
In acts so small, yet full of grace.
For kindness flows, a river wide,
In every heart, it will abide.

Curves of Compassion

In gentle arcs and flowing lines,
Compassion whispers, softly shines.
Embracing pain, in others' hearts,
With every curve, a healing starts.

Around the world, a tender touch,
Healing wounds that hurt so much.
In every tear, a bittersweet,
Compassion finds its rhythmic beat.

Where curves collide, the warmth unites,
In every soul, a spark ignites.
In quiet moments, we just see,
The strength in love when hearts agree.

Through storms of doubt, we stand our ground,
In curves of hope, love can be found.
We'll lift each other, hand in hand,
In every curve, together stand.

Compassion flows like rivers wide,
In every heart, it will reside.
A sacred bond, our spirits share,
In softest curves, we learn to care.

Lines of Loyalty

In paths we tread, where trust is formed,
Loyal hearts, through trials warmed.
Each line we trace, a promise made,
In shadows deep, our bonds won't fade.

Through every storm, we stand as one,
With steadfast hearts, our battle's won.
In shared laughter and quiet sighs,
Loyalty blooms, as time flies.

A compass true, when roads are rough,
In every trial, we'll be enough.
With every line that we do write,
Our loyalty glows, a guiding light.

Across the miles, our paths aligned,
In loyalty's arms, our love defined.
With each new day, our hearts engage,
Each line we draw, a new page.

So here we stand, in harmony,
Each line a pledge, a symphony.
Together strong, through thick and thin,
In lines of loyalty, we begin.

Triangles of Trust

In corners formed, relationships grow,
Triangles of trust, where love can flow.
With every side, a strength defined,
In sacred bonds, our hearts entwined.

Three points of light, in unity,
Together we rise, in harmony.
With laughter shared and secrets kept,
In trust we build, the dreams we've wept.

Through trials faced, we stand so tall,
In triangles strong, we'll never fall.
With every angle, carefully drawn,
In trust we flourish, a brand new dawn.

When shadows creep, and doubts arise,
In triangles of trust, our faith won't die.
We lift each other, hand in hand,
In every challenge, on love we stand.

So here's to bonds that never break,
In triangles formed, our hearts awake.
With every side, we stand so true,
In trust, we find the best of you.

Coordinates of Care

In the map of hearts we trace,
Every kindness finds its place.
Gentle gestures, softly shared,
In this world, love is declared.

Hope illuminates the night,
Guiding us to what is right.
With each smile, a spark ignites,
Binding souls in shared delights.

Hands that reach through silent tears,
Whisper comfort, calm our fears.
In the giving, we find grace,
Threads of faith in warm embrace.

Through the storms, we stand as one,
Shadows passing, battles won.
In this journey, we explore,
Coordinates lead us to the more.

With compassion as our guide,
In our hearts, we take great pride.
For in nurturing, we live,
To the world, our love we give.

Pulse of Promises

Every heartbeat sings its song,
In the rhythm, we belong.
Trust and hope in every vow,
Promises made, we cherish now.

The gentle whispers fill the air,
Soft commitments everywhere.
In our dreams, a future waits,
Crafted by the love we create.

With each pledge, a bond grows strong,
Carried with us all along.
Together we can brave the night,
Guided by that inner light.

Even when the road gets rough,
We will find our way, it's tough.
With our hearts in sync, we'll soar,
In the pulse, we will find more.

Hold the visions close and dear,
In our dance, we banish fear.
For in promise lies the key,
Unlocking what we're meant to be.

Harmonies in Hugs

In the warmth where spirits meet,
Every embrace, a rhythmic beat.
Silent symphonies we share,
Melodies that lift the air.

With each hug, a story told,
In the fabric, love unfolds.
Gentle touch and tender sighs,
Creating peace where comfort lies.

Wrapped in arms, we find our way,
Through the night, into the day.
In the bond, our hearts align,
Intertwined like the sweetest vine.

Softest echoes fill the space,
In these moments, we find grace.
With a squeeze, our fears release,
In the hug, we find our peace.

Together, we can face the storm,
In this shelter, hearts keep warm.
In the harmony of affection,
We discover deep connection.

Portraits of Patience

In the stillness, we must stand,
Time unfolds with gentle hand.
Brush of love on canvas bare,
Each stroke tells of hope and care.

Growing roots in tender ground,
In the waiting, strength is found.
Each moment like a painted hue,
Crafting lives so rich and true.

With the passing of the days,
In the quiet, wisdom plays.
Each heartbeat echoes softly, slow,
In the patience, love will grow.

Layers build in softest light,
Through the dark, we find our sight.
Portraits filled with joy and tears,
Capturing the dance of years.

Every chapter tells a tale,
In each challenge, we prevail.
With the brush of time's embrace,
We create our sacred space.

Threads of Thoughtfulness

In the quiet moments, we weave,
Threads of kindness, we believe.
Each stitch a word, softly said,
Embracing hearts where love is spread.

In the tapestry of day and night,
Thoughts connect, a gentle light.
Woven dreams that softly glow,
Guiding us where we must go.

With every thread, a story spun,
Life's tapestry has just begun.
Interlaced with hope and care,
A fabric rich, beyond compare.

Through the loom of time we send,
Wishes warm that never end.
Threads entwined in unity,
Creating bonds, setting us free.

In the end, we all shall find,
The thoughts we've shared have intertwined.
As we gather, our hearts shall hum,
In this fabric, we become one.

Seeds of Sincerity

Plant the seeds of truth and grace,
In every heart, in every space.
Water them with gentle care,
Watch them bloom, beyond compare.

In the garden of open hearts,
Sincerity is where it starts.
Nurtured by the sun's warm light,
Growing strong, reaching for heights.

Through storms and trials, they withstand,
With roots so deep, they understand.
Whispers of love among the leaves,
In their embrace, the spirit believes.

Harvest comes, a rewarding yield,
In the soil, our truths revealed.
Gather round, the fruits we share,
Seeds of sincerity everywhere.

With every season, let them grow,
A legacy that we all know.
From small beginnings, great things soar,
Together, we can strive for more.

Ribbons of Respect

Ribbons flowing in the breeze,
Symbolizing what we seize.
Respect for all, a sacred thread,
Raising voices for the unsaid.

In every meeting, in every gaze,
A ribbon bright in many ways.
Binding us with empathy,
In this dance of harmony.

With each honor that we bestow,
Ribbons of kindness gently flow.
Ties that bind us, strong and true,
Mutual regard in all we do.

As we honor, hearts combine,
Ribbons of respect intertwine.
Draped across our shared endeavor,
In unity, we stand forever.

At the end, as we reflect,
Love and kindness we select.
Together, let our spirits sail,
Ribbons of respect prevail.

Dances of Devotion

In the moonlight, shadows play,
Dances of love light the way.
Every step, a promise made,
In devotion, hearts cascade.

Through the rhythm, souls align,
In this dance, your hand in mine.
Spinning dreams under the stars,
Boundless love, no distance bars.

With each twirl, we find our place,
In devotion's warm embrace.
A tapestry of years gone by,
Every heartbeat, a heartfelt sigh.

As the music softly swells,
In our hearts, a story dwells.
Dancing through the highs and lows,
Together, our devotion grows.

At daybreak, as we stand still,
In our hearts, the love we feel.
Forevermore, through time's great flow,
In dances of devotion, we will go.

Connected by Threads

In the fabric of our days,
We weave our lives so fine,
Each thread a silent story,
Entwined by fate's design.

Moments stitched together,
In colors rich and bright,
Binding hearts with echoes,
Of laughter, love, and light.

Through storms and sunny skies,
Our tapestry unfolds,
With every shared connection,
A tale of warmth that holds.

With distant paths but close minds,
We find a common ground,
In the pulling of these threads,
A bond forever found.

Together we create,
A quilt of cherished dreams,
Each patch a memory made,
In life's intricate seams.

The Topography of Thoughtfulness

In valleys deep of silence,
Thoughts wander and explore,
Mountains rise of kindness,
With each heart open door.

Rivers of reflection flow,
Carving pathways in the mind,
Every stone a moment,
A glimpse of truth defined.

Fields of empathy stretch wide,
With blooms of understanding,
Nature's map of giving,
In every heart's demanding.

The skyline holds potential,
As stars align above,
In this vast topography,
We navigate with love.

With each step of intention,
We trace our way anew,
In the landscape of our thoughts,
Together, we break through.

Subtle Angles of Awareness

In the stillness of the moment,
A whisper touches soul,
Awareness dances lightly,
As shadows start to roll.

Glimmers of perception,
In every fleeting glance,
The subtle bends of knowing,
In this quiet dance.

Fragments of the larger truth,
Pieced through gentle care,
Awareness in the angles,
Where silence fills the air.

In the labyrinth of feeling,
Each corner holds a clue,
The angles shift with learning,
In the light of what is true.

With every breath and heartbeat,
We carve the path of grace,
Subtle angles bridge our worlds,
In this sacred space.

The Frame of Shared Silence

Across the room, we linger,
In a stillness that connects,
A frame of quiet presence,
Where words are but mere specs.

In the hush, our hearts converse,
In each unspoken thought,
The silence speaks of solace,
In the moments that we've sought.

Time slows as we sit still,
The world outside may fade,
In this shared cocoon of peace,
Our souls are gently laid.

Each breath a shared rhythm,
In the calm we call our own,
Within this frame of silence,
True understanding's grown.

Together in this quiet,
We find a sacred truth,
In the frame that holds our silence,
Eternal bonds of youth.

Arcs of Affection

In gentle curves our hearts entwine,
Beneath the stars, your hand in mine.
Each whisper soft, a tender trace,
In every glance, a warm embrace.

Through trials faced, our spirits rise,
Like sunlit dawns in painted skies.
Together strong, we forge our way,
A bond that time cannot betray.

As seasons change, our love extends,
In laughter shared, in moments spent.
With every smile, our spirits lift,
In simple things, our greatest gift.

When shadows fall, we find our light,
With every heartbeat, pure delight.
In arcs of grace, our souls align,
A journey blessed by love divine.

Dimensions of Devotion

In every glance, a silent vow,
In quiet spaces, here and now.
Together woven, thread by thread,
In dreams we share, where hopes are spread.

Through every storm and gentle breeze,
Our hearts are anchored, finding ease.
In laughter's echo, and tears we shed,
In the sacred spaces where love is fed.

A canvas wide, painted with trust,
In golden hues, our hearts adjust.
With every heartbeat, rhythm flows,
In dreams we write, our love bestows.

In gentle whispers, truth unfolds,
In stories shared, our lives are told.
Each moment lived, in love's embrace,
Dimensions vast, a sacred place.

Chords of Connection

In softest notes, our hearts compose,
A melody where love bestows.
With every touch, a harmony,
In chords of trust, you dance with me.

As time unfolds, we play our song,
In rhythms sweet, we both belong.
Each laughter shared, a vibrant tune,
In twilight's glow, beneath the moon.

With whispers low, we strike a chord,
In woven dreams, our souls afford.
In every glance, a spark ignites,
In music's flow, our love takes flight.

In grand crescendos, we rise and fall,
A timeless tune that binds us all.
Chords of connection, pure and true,
In every beat, it leads to you.

Patterns in the Heart

In quiet moments where shadows play,
Patterns weave in a tender sway.
With every laugh, a thread imposed,
In love's rich tapestry, we're enclosed.

As seasons shift, the fabric blends,
In vibrant hues, our journey bends.
Each color shared, a story spun,
In patterns drawn, two souls as one.

In echoes soft, a rhythm found,
In whispered dreams, our hopes surround.
By fireside glow, and starlit nights,
Patterns emerge, our hearts take flight.

Through trials faced, we weave anew,
In every challenge, love shines through.
A legacy built, in time we'll chart,
In intricate patterns, within the heart.

Facades of Fearlessness

Brave masks worn in the night,
Hiding hearts that feel in fright.
Battles fought behind closed doors,
Strength displayed, yet silence roars.

Shadows dance where doubts reside,
Glimmers of hope they try to hide.
Courage builds on fragile ground,
In the stillness, truth is found.

Whispers challenge the bravest soul,
A facade crafted to feel whole.
Yet cracks appear as courage fades,
In the light, the mask parades.

Voices echo through the dark,
Each brave act ignites a spark.
The fragile heart beneath the skin,
Seeks the strength to fight within.

Fearlessness wears many hats,
Pretendings, illusions, like acrobats.
Yet in the quiet, strength is real,
Facades lifting, hearts can heal.

Weavings of Wonder

Threads of dreams in twilight spun,
Wrapping the world in magic fun.
Colors blend where hearts entwine,
Each moment makes our spirits shine.

In the garden of the mind,
Nature's beauty, brightly lined.
Petals whisper tales untold,
Secrets woven, brave and bold.

Skyward glances, stars ignite,
With every wish, a new delight.
Wonder flows like rivers wide,
In every soul, it must reside.

Every heartbeat sings a song,
In the fabric where we belong.
Stitching love with joy and grace,
Together we can find our place.

Weaving moments, large and small,
In the tapestry, we learn to fall.
From wonder's loom, we craft our fate,
In the threads of life, we celebrate.

Palettes of Peace

Soft hues blend in morning light,
Gentle whispers calm the night.
Each stroke of color, warm and true,
Creates a world where hope breaks through.

Silence drapes the earth so wide,
In stillness, hearts find a guide.
Pastel skies and tranquil seas,
Breathe in harmony; feel the ease.

Fields of gold and azure skies,
Nature's art, where freedom flies.
Every shade a soothing balm,
In the chaos, find the calm.

Mellow browns and greens of earth,
In every tone, we find our worth.
Brush of kindness paints the day,
In peace we learn to find our way.

Palette rich with love and grace,
Every color, a warm embrace.
In this canvas, together we stand,
Creating peace, hand in hand.

Hues of Humanity

In every face a story lies,
A canvas of laughter, love, and cries.
Each hue speaks of joy and pain,
In the light, we dance, we gain.

Shades of hope and shades of fear,
In harmony, we draw them near.
An artist's vision, pure and bright,
Illuminates our shared plight.

Brushstrokes bold in varied colors,
Unity found in diverse wonders.
No two shades can ever be wrong,
Together we create a song.

Melodies of kindness shared,
In this world, no heart should be bared.
Each hue a testament to believe,
In our colors, we learn to weave.

Humanity's vibrant, rich tapestry,
In every thread, our history.
Bound by love, in harmony's glow,
In the hues of humanity, we grow.

Chords of Conscientiousness

In whispers soft, the heart does speak,
A gentle pulse, where shadows peek.
Each thought a note, each breath a tune,
In harmony beneath the moon.

Within the mind, a symphony,
Of hopes entwined, and journeys free.
A chord of peace, a soothing sound,
In every soul, this truth is found.

The echoes rise, a melody,
Through every pain, through every plea.
In every fret, in every strain,
We find our joy, we learn from pain.

Together strong, we sing as one,
A tapestry, bright as the sun.
With every beat, we come alive,
In chords of care, our spirits thrive.

The path of love, the road of grace,
We walk along, a sacred space.
In every strum, a truth revealed,
In diligent hearts, our fates are sealed.

Vectors of Vulnerability

In moments raw, the truth unfolds,
A fragile heart, a story told.
Through tears that fall, we brave the night,
With open arms, we greet the light.

The lines we draw, so faint, so fine,
In every crack, the stars align.
With brave-faced flaws, we find our way,
In honest words, we dare to stay.

Each scar a tale, of battles fought,
In silent whispers, battles wrought.
With every breath, we take the leap,
In vulnerability, emotions seep.

Together we stand, in strength found new,
This intimate dance, a vital view.
In shared confessions, we break the mold,
And weave the warmth from threads of gold.

In trusting souls, we find our peace,
A fleeting touch, a sweet release.
With gentle hands, we build the bridge,
In vectors true, love does not hedge.

Dimensions of Delight

In playful light, the laughter glows,
In every moment, joy bestows.
The colors bloom, like spring anew,
In every heart, the joy rings true.

In dancing leaves, the breezes play,
Each sunrise casts a golden ray.
In shared embraces, warmth ignites,
In kindness found, the spirit fights.

With every smile, the world expands,
In simple gestures, love commands.
Where worry fades, and hope takes flight,
In every glance, the dream feels right.

Through whispered words, the magic weaves,
In cozy nooks, the heart believes.
In flavors rich, in stories spun,
In every dream, we are as one.

A canvas wide, with colors bright,
In joyful tones, we find our light.
In this vast space, delight resides,
In shared souls twined, love never hides.

The Horizon of Human Souls

Beyond the dusk, where dreams take flight,
A horizon glows with soft, pure light.
In every face, a story gleams,
In every gaze, the hope redeems.

The skies unfold, in colors vast,
A tapestry of futures cast.
With open hearts, we seek the dawn,
In unity, our fears are gone.

Through every tear, the wisdom grows,
In every laugh, the spirit flows.
Together here, our voices rise,
In shared compassion, truth defies.

From distant shores, our journeys meet,
In every step, the pulse, the beat.
With arms outstretched, we break the bounds,
In every soul, the love surrounds.

The future calls, with vibrant grace,
In every heart, a sacred space.
As we embrace, the shadows fade,
In the horizon, our hopes are laid.

The Measure of a Moment

In a heartbeat, life can change,
Seconds linger, rearrange.
Time's whisper on the skin,
Moments lost, yet found within.

A glance shared, a smile bright,
Fleeting shadows, pure delight.
Echoes of laughter ring clear,
Memories held, forever dear.

The ticking clock, a soft call,
In silence, we can feel it all.
Glimpses deep, the world in pause,
In stillness, we find our cause.

Between the breaths, a spark ignites,
In the depths of endless nights.
Every glance, a tale unfolds,
In every heartbeat, love retold.

Moments merge, as rivers flow,
In the now, we learn to grow.
Each instant, a precious gift,
In life's dance, we find our drift.

Harmonies of Human Touch

Fingers entwined, a silent song,
In the hush, where hearts belong.
A warm embrace, the world fades,
In the space where love cascades.

The brush of skin, a gentle spark,
In the daylight, through the dark.
Voices soft, entwined like vines,
In the warmth, the spirit shines.

Each hug, a language all its own,
In every touch, we are shown.
The power held in tender hands,
Uniting souls, where love expands.

With every kiss, the world dissolves,
In this bond, our hearts resolve.
Connection deep, beyond the sight,
In human touch, we find our light.

Moments shared, a symphony,
In the dance of you and me.
Through every heartbeat, truth we find,
In love's embrace, we are aligned.

The Structure of Solace

In shadows' reach, comfort grows,
A refuge found, where nothing goes.
With whispered dreams and quiet sighs,
The heart's retreat beneath the skies.

Walls built strong from weary days,
In stillness, the spirit sways.
Cloaked in calm, the world recedes,
As hope and peace plant gentle seeds.

A sacred space, where thoughts can roam,
In every breath, we find our home.
Soft winds carry burdens away,
In solace found, broken hearts stay.

The architecture of our fears,
In tender light, the solace clears.
Every crack, a story shared,
In healing, we know we've dared.

Together we build, one heart's beat,
In every step, a soft retreat.
The structure holds, a bond profound,
In shared solace, love is found.

Reflections in a Broken Mirror

Fragments cast in silvered light,
Shattered pieces spark the night.
In disarray, we seek the whole,
In reflections, we find our soul.

Each shard tells a tale untold,
In broken glass, memories fold.
The past lingers in every gleam,
A mosaic of our silent dream.

Faces blur in the scattered glass,
In each moment, we see the past.
The beauty lies in what is lost,
In chaos, we learn to count the cost.

Through jagged edges, truths arise,
In splintered hopes, we recognize.
Every fracture, a chance to mend,
In broken mirrors, we begin to blend.

We gather pieces, rebuild our hearts,
In every crack, a new path starts.
Reflections dance, in light they sway,
In a broken mirror, we find our way.

Pillars of Positivity

In the glow of each sunrise,
Hope paints the sky anew.
Whispers of courage arise,
Chasing away the blue.

With every kind word shared,
We build a bridge of light.
Together, we have fared,
Finding strength in the fight.

Through shadows that may loom,
We stand hand in hand strong.
In the heart, there's room,
For the joy in our song.

Each moment, we create,
A tapestry of grace.
Love conquers all fate,
In this shared, safe space.

From pillars that won't sway,
Our spirits ever high.
Together, come what may,
We reach for the sky.

Tides of Togetherness

Like waves that kiss the shore,
We gather, hand in hand.
In harmony, we soar,
Together we will stand.

The currents may shift fast,
Yet our bond holds tight.
With each storm that has passed,
We move towards the light.

In laughter and in tears,
We share the highs and lows.
Defeating all our fears,
In the warmth love bestows.

United, we are strong,
Our hearts, a rhythmic beat.
No place feels like we belong,
Like the tides beneath our feet.

As one, we find our way,
Through all that life may bring.
In every single day,
Together we will sing.

Vistas of Valor

In valleys deep and wide,
Bravery takes its flight.
With courage as our guide,
We rise to meet the night.

Mountains stand tall and proud,
Echoing our fierce heart.
Within the starlit crowd,
We find where we can start.

In battles fought with grace,
We uncover our might.
With each challenge we face,
We emerge from the fight.

Vistas stretch before us,
With dreams that touch the sky.
Together, without fuss,
We dare to reach up high.

With valor lighting the way,
We chase the dawn's sweet glow.
In unity, we sway,
As we embrace the flow.

Waves of Warmth

Upon the shores of life,
Love's waves crash ever near.
Through moments filled with strife,
Our hearts grow ever clear.

Embracing sunlit days,
We bask in joy's warm light.
With laughter's sweet displays,
We chase away the night.

The tides of friendship swell,
Reminding us we're one.
In stories shared, we tell,
Of battles lost and won.

Together, side by side,
We weather every storm.
In unity, we stride,
In each other's warmth, warm.

As waves roll in and out,
We dance upon the sand.
In love, we have no doubt,
Together, hand in hand.

Cascades of Comfort

In gentle flows, the waters gleam,
Whispers soft like a tender dream.
Each ripple sings a soothing tune,
Beneath the watchful light of the moon.

Nestled in the arms of the night,
Cascading joys take endless flight.
Embraces warm as summer's breath,
A haven found, transcending death.

Through valleys deep, where shadows play,
Comfort calls, dispelling gray.
With every drop, a memory falls,
In the quiet, love gently calls.

The mountains echo, high and grand,
As flows of peace sweep through the land.
Rivers carve the stones of pain,
In their embrace, hope will remain.

So let the waters guide your heart,
In cascades of comfort, never apart.
For in each wave that meets the shore,
Lies a promise, forevermore.

Steps of Support

With every step, we stand in place,
Hand in hand, a warm embrace.
Through winding paths and trials faced,
Together, strength is gently traced.

In silent moments, we can share,
The weight of burdens, light as air.
Each footfall echoes resolve anew,
A steadfast bond, reliable and true.

Together we rise, hearts intertwined,
With love's assurance, brightly aligned.
Through storms we weather, side by side,
In steps of support, we shall not hide.

In laughter's light or sorrow's shade,
The journey is richer, not afraid.
Though the road may twist, we trust the way,
In every moment, by each other's stay.

As we tread the path of dreams not yet told,
We're woven in stories, brave and bold.
Each step, a heartbeat, a promise made,
In the tapestry of life, we're lovingly laid.

Shadows of Sympathy

In twilight's hush, where sorrows blend,
The shadows linger, eager to mend.
Soft gazes shared beneath the night,
In silence speaks a kindred light.

With every breath, empathy flows,
In the quiet where understanding grows.
Through whispered hope in darkest hours,
We find resilience, blooming flowers.

Beneath the weight of unspoken fears,
We gather strength through our shared tears.
Compassion wraps us in its embrace,
In shadows of sympathy, we find grace.

Together we wander, hand in hand,
In unison, united we stand.
For in each echo, a voice remains,
A reminder that love always sustains.

So let the shadows tell their tale,
Of hearts entwined, we shall not fail.
For in the dark, a spark ignites,
Guiding us through the longest nights.

Currents of Courage

In the depths of fear, a light resides,
Coursing through waves, where hope abides.
A gentle push, a spark within,
Currents of courage, where we begin.

Each surge of strength against the tide,
A fierce resolve we cannot hide.
Through raging storms and crashing waves,
We learn to dance, to be as brave.

With every challenge that we face,
Courage flows, a warm embrace.
Together we navigate the unknown,
In currents shared, we've truly grown.

For in the struggle, we find our wings,
Lost in the rhythm that nature sings.
With hearts united, we break the mold,
In currents of courage, we rise bold.

So let the waters crash and roar,
With every swell, we seek for more.
In this vast ocean, we find our way,
Currents of courage guide our day.

Patterns Amidst Chaos

In swirling storms of wild designs,
Fleeting shapes in tangled lines.
Chaos dances, yet finds a way,
To craft a rhythm that will sway.

Colors clash and shadows play,
Each moment whispers, 'Stay your way.'
A tapestry of dreams unfurled,
Patterns woven through the world.

In every twist, a story told,
Mysteries wrapped, yet to unfold.
Chaos sings, a bold refrain,
In patterns formed from joy and pain.

Underneath the vibrant strife,
A pulse that echoes, hints at life.
Found in cracks where light breaks through,
Beauty born from shades of blue.

Here in the midst of wild despair,
Patterns shimmer in the air.
Hold on tight to what you find,
In chaos, heart and mind aligned.

Triangles of Trust

In corners where the shadows blend,
Three sides meet; they start to mend.
A bond created, sharp and clear,
Trust builds strong as we draw near.

Each angle forms a whispered pact,
With open hearts, there's no act.
In gentle curves of time and space,
We find our way, embrace our grace.

Through storms we stand, a steady base,
Unyielding hearts, a warm embrace.
The distance fades, we stand as one,
In triangles of trust, we've won.

Together we pen a tale so bright,
Illuminated through darkest night.
With every step, we rise and soar,
Triangles of trust forevermore.

Each bond a path, a guiding line,
In shapes of love, our spirits align.
We hold the truth in every thrust,
In life's embrace, in triangles of trust.

The Symmetry of a Smile

In gentle curves, a warmth ignites,
Symmetry in the soft delights.
A smile that bridges space and time,
Creating joy, a sweet rhyme.

With every turn of lips that rise,
A mirror held to sparkling eyes.
In perfect balance, moments meet,
In every grin, the world's heartbeat.

Through mirrored faces, love we share,
A symmetry beyond compare.
In laughter's echo, dreams take flight,
The simple joy, pure and bright.

Each shared glance, a silent vow,
In smiles, we find our sacred now.
The world may spin, yet we remain,
In symmetry, alive and sane.

So let your smile be a shining light,
Illuminating shadows of the night.
For in this act, our spirits climb,
Embracing life in perfect rhyme.

The Edge of Empathy

At the boundary where hearts collide,
We surface truths we often hide.
Waves of understanding flow,
At the edge where feelings grow.

Each pulse and breath a shared embrace,
In our worlds, we find a place.
The edge is sharp, but soft to touch,
A reminder that we're all loved much.

In listening lies a sacred art,
To feel the ache within the heart.
A bridge between what's yours and mine,
On this edge, our souls align.

With every story shared out loud,
In tenderness, we're sorely proud.
Beneath the weight of unspoke fears,
Empathy wipes away the tears.

So let us gather on this line,
With open hearts, our paths entwine.
For in the understanding we possess,
We find true strength, we find our best.

Echoes of Encouragement

In shadows cast by doubt's embrace,
A whisper grows, a gentle grace.
With every fear, we rise and stand,
A brighter path, a guiding hand.

Through valleys deep, and mountains high,
Our spirits soar, they cannot die.
Resilience blooms in every heart,
Together strong, we're never apart.

When storms arise and hope feels thin,
We'll face the waves, we'll learn to swim.
With voices loud, we'll sing our song,
In unity, where we belong.

The spark within shall never fade,
In every step, foundations laid.
With courage found, we'll rise anew,
The echoes loud, our strength is true.

For every trial we face today,
The light will guide, show us the way.
In echoes sweet, we find our call,
Together we shall never fall.

Veins of Validation

The truth runs deep, like rivers wide,
In every pulse, our hearts abide.
With every word, we find our face,
In tender courage, we embrace.

A tapestry of thoughts entwined,
In every shadow, light we'll find.
Through spoken dreams and silent fears,
The veins of life flow through the years.

To chase the doubts that linger near,
With every breath, we brush the fear.
Validation in each thread spun,
Together, we are ever one.

In every laugh, and every tear,
A testament of those held dear.
The journey shared, a bond so strong,
In truth, we rise, where hearts belong.

So let them speak, the tales of old,
In every moment, brave and bold.
For through these veins, our stories flow,
And in validation, we shall grow.

Lines of Longing

In whispered dreams, the night unfolds,
A tale of hearts, a longing bold.
Like distant stars, we've lost our way,
Yet hope remains, the light of day.

We write our lines on parchment frayed,
In ink of love, our fears displayed.
Each stroke a promise, deep and vast,
In ink of time, our shadows cast.

Across the miles, the silence hums,
In every beat, a yearning comes.
For connection sought in fleeting breath,
In quiet hope, defying death.

With every glance, a spark ignites,
A bridge of souls, through endless nights.
In every word, a thread we weave,
Lines of longing, we believe.

So let us chase these dreams anew,
With hearts unbound, together through.
In every line, our stories blend,
In longing's arms, we find the end.

Threads of Truth

In woven hearts, the truth entwines,
Through every doubt, a light defines.
Unraveled tales of love and pain,
In honest threads, we break the chain.

With fabric soft as evening's sigh,
We stitch our dreams, we learn to fly.
Each knot a lesson, deeply forged,
In every tear, a hope engorged.

Through tangled paths and twisted roads,
We carry burdens, share the loads.
In every voice, the whisper grows,
The truth unveils, as beauty shows.

We seek the light that guides our way,
With threads of truth, we find our stay.
In unity, our hearts will weave,
Through laughter shared, we shall believe.

In silent nights and waking dawns,
Our stories blend, like dusk to morn.
With every breath, we'll honor these,
Threads of truth that aim to please.

Intersections of Insight

In twilight's gleam, thoughts collide,
Paths entwined, where wisdom's tried.
Echoes whisper, softly call,
In the silence, we stand tall.

Veils of doubt begin to lift,
Finding light, a precious gift.
Each moment's breath, a chance to see,
The beauty in our unity.

Questions flicker like distant stars,
Mapping dreams, despite our scars.
Every choice, a thread we weave,
In this tapestry, we believe.

Through the maze, we navigate,
In every soul, we resonate.
With open hearts and mindful ways,
We gather strength in shared rays.

At crossroads, we dare to pause,
Seeing selves in nature's laws.
From every struggle, we unwind,
Finding truth in love entwined.

Symphonies of Solace

In gentle hush, the night descends,
Where quietude and peace transcends.
Each heartbeat sings a humble tune,
Underneath the silver moon.

Whispers greet the morning light,
As shadows fade, we take flight.
The world awakens, fresh and new,
In serene notes, we find what's true.

Harmony flows through every soul,
Binding hearts to feel whole.
With every breath, a chance to heal,
Revealing truths that we conceal.

In the storms, we find our grace,
Lost and found in love's embrace.
Together, in this sacred space,
We discover solace, find our place.

As the echoes linger on,
In symphonies of dusk and dawn,
With open arms, we welcome change,
In every note, life's grand exchange.

Points of Positivity

Amidst the noise, a gentle nudge,
A reminder to not begrudge.
In every trial, a lesson learned,
Flames of hope, forever burned.

Every smile, a spark of light,
Turning darkness into bright.
With each kind word that we share,
We build a world that's free from care.

In laughter, we find common ground,
Together, our voices resound.
Moments cherished, like sweet refrain,
In unity, we break the chain.

Through challenges, we rise and stand,
In every heart, a helping hand.
With gratitude, we craft our way,
In points of joy, we choose to stay.

As we gather, side by side,
In every tear, a spark of pride.
With open eyes, we see the light,
In life's journey, everything feels right.

Swirls of Sentiment

In colored hues, emotions blend,
A dance of feelings, without end.
From deep within, a story flows,
In every heartbeat, the beauty grows.

The gentle touch of autumn's breeze,
Whispers sweet, in rustling leaves.
From distant shores, we feel the call,
In swirls of love, we rise and fall.

Through every smile, a world opens wide,
A canvas painted, side by side.
In laughter's echo, we find release,
In heartfelt moments, we taste peace.

With memory's brush, we softly weave,
Tales of warmth, in hearts we believe.
Each sentiment, a treasure stored,
In swirls of kindness, we are adored.

As seasons shift, emotions shift too,
In every hue, a love so true.
Navigating life with open hearts,
In swirls of sentiment, beauty starts.

Grids of Gratitude

In the tapestry of dawn, we rise,
Counting blessings, bright as skies.
Every smile, a stitch we weave,
In grateful hearts, we truly believe.

Moments shared, like stars aligned,
Illuminating paths we find.
A gentle touch, a soft embrace,
In gratitude, we find our place.

Fields of kindness bloom and grow,
In every seed of love we sow.
Echoes of laughter fill the air,
In grids of gratitude, we share.

Each whisper of the wind, a song,
Reminding us where we belong.
Through trials faced, we hold on tight,
In hearts of gratitude, we ignite.

So let us paint with colors bright,
A canvas filled with sheer delight.
With every heartbeat, let it show,
In grids of gratitude, we glow.

Designs of Daring

On the edge where shadows dance,
We embrace every bold chance.
With every step, we break the mold,
In designs of daring, we're brave and bold.

Dreams unfurl like banners high,
Chasing visions that touch the sky.
With open hearts and minds set free,
In courageous paths, we dare to be.

Each risk taken, a story born,
From the darkness, we rise at dawn.
In the face of fears, our spirits climb,
In designs of daring, we stretch through time.

With fiery hearts, we forge ahead,
In the whispers of hope, we're led.
Together we stand, unafraid to roam,
In designs of daring, we build our home.

So let us dive into the unknown,
In the tapestry of dreams, we've sewn.
Hand in hand, through storms we'll steer,
In designs of daring, we persevere.

Frames of Friendship

In frames of laughter, memories cling,
Like melodies that softly sing.
Each moment captured, pure and true,
In the art of friendship, me and you.

Through seasons change, our bond stays bright,
Warming hearts like morning light.
In every glance, a story shared,
In frames of friendship, we've always cared.

A gentle word, a comforting hug,
In the corners where our lives jug.
Frames adorned with trust and cheer,
In friendship's embrace, we hold dear.

Through trials faced and joys we've known,
In the tapestry of life, we've grown.
Together we paint our vivid dreams,
In frames of friendship, love redeems.

So let us cherish every part,
Crafting portraits from the heart.
With colors rich, and hues so bright,
In frames of friendship, we unite.

Mosaics of Memory

In a garden where shadows fall,
We gather pieces, great and small.
Each fragment tells a whispered tale,
In mosaics of memory, we set sail.

Time's gentle brush paints the past,
Moments captured, forever cast.
In colors bold and shades so rare,
In mosaics of memory, we declare.

Through laughter bright and tears that flow,
Each memory, a seed we sow.
In the patterns of love we see,
In mosaics of memory, you and me.

Together we weave a vibrant scene,
Of cherished times that glow and glean.
In every shard, a part of us glows,
In mosaics of memory, our love grows.

So let us frame this timeless art,
Holding each piece close to the heart.
With every glance, we find our glee,
In mosaics of memory, we are free.

Echoes of Empathy

In shadows soft, our voices blend,
A gentle touch, to hearts we send.
In silence, echoes start to weave,
The threads of hope that we believe.

With every tear, a story shared,
Of pain and joy, each moment bared.
Together strong, we face the night,
In unity, we find the light.

Through storms we walk, hand in hand,
Each step we take, a frail demand.
Yet in our grip, the warmth remains,
An endless bond that softens pains.

With listening hearts, we find our way,
Through tangled paths, come what may.
For every soul holds tales untold,
In empathy, our treasures unfold.

In whispered dreams, hope takes its flight,
We rise together, bound by sight.
To others' needs, we pledge our stay,
In echoes sweet, we guide the way.

Grains of Generosity

In fields of giving, seeds are sown,
Each grain a gift, in love it's grown.
With open hearts, we share our time,
In every act, we create a rhyme.

The smallest gesture lights the way,
A smile exchanged, brightens the day.
In kindness found, our spirits dance,
Each humble act, a second chance.

Through hands that lift, and voices kind,
We plant the hope that we can find.
In every heart, a spark ignites,
For generosity takes its flights.

A listening ear, a warm embrace,
In tender moments, we find our place.
The grains of love, in abundance spread,
A legacy of good ahead.

With every meal that we prepare,
And every thought, we choose to share.
In gratitude, our hearts will sing,
For grains of joy that kindness brings.

Weaver's Wisdom

In twilight's glow, the weaver sighs,
With threads of hope that never dies.
Each strand a lesson, firm and true,
In fabric bright, a world anew.

With deft hands, the weaver spins,
The tales of life where love begins.
In every pattern, stories thread,
From joy to pain, all gently spread.

Through vibrant hues, the past is shown,
The wisdom gained, the seeds we've sown.
For each mistake, a path redesigned,
In woven tales, our hearts aligned.

The loom of life, with trials vast,
In each design, we learn from past.
Through every tear, a patch we sew,
And from the scars, new strength will grow.

So gather 'round, let stories flow,
In weaver's art, we come to know.
For through the threads, our truths reside,
In wisdom's weave, we all abide.

Bridges of Benevolence

In every heart, a bridge is laid,
A path of light through dark we wade.
With arms outstretched, we join as one,
In acts of care, all fears undone.

The bridges built on trust and grace,
Uniting souls in this vast space.
Through kindness shown, we pave the way,
For peace and love to come and stay.

In tender words, we find our spark,
Illuminating shadows dark.
Together strong, we rise and stand,
In benevolence, we lend a hand.

In moments shared, we stitch the seams,
Creating hope from shattered dreams.
For every heart that dares to reach,
Is strengthened by the love we teach.

So let us walk these bridges wide,
In unity, we will abide.
With open hearts, let's share the load,
For benevolence lights our road.

Configurations of Compassion

In soft whispers of the night,
Hearts awaken pure and bright.
A gentle touch, a knowing glance,
Together lost in tranquil dance.

Through struggles shared and burdens light,
Compassion blooms, a guiding light.
Hands entwined in silent prayer,
A bond so deep, beyond compare.

With every word, a soothing balm,
In storms of life, we find our calm.
A tapestry of love we weave,
In this embrace, we truly believe.

Through trials faced, our spirits rise,
Beneath the weight of weary skies.
With every heartbeat, closer drawn,
Compassion's song, our hearts have sworn.

So let us forge through darkest nights,
In every pain, our hope ignites.
Together strong, together free,
In configurations, you and me.

Forming Bonds in Shadows

In quiet corners, shadows blend,
Mysteries shared with an unseen friend.
Whispers floating on the breeze,
In muted laughter, we find ease.

The world may dim, the lights may fade,
Yet in the night, our hearts are laid.
Through secret smiles and knowing winks,
In such moments, the bond strengthens.

Beneath the stars, stories unfold,
In every silence, secrets told.
With open hearts, we dare to see,
The beauty that in shadows can be.

Each fleeting glance, a spark ignites,
In shared stillness, our souls take flight.
From darkened paths, we find the way,
Forming bonds that forever stay.

So let us walk where shadows lie,
In quiet strength, together try.
For in the dusk, love's magic grows,
In forming bonds, the heart bestows.

The Art of Subtle Touch

A brush of fingers, soft and light,
In moments fleeting, pure delight.
With every graze, a spark ignites,
In tenderness, the spirit fights.

The simple act, a silent grace,
In every meeting, a warm embrace.
In subtle ways, emotions flow,
A language rich, we come to know.

With careful steps, we navigate,
In gentle strokes, we celebrate.
The art of touch, profound and true,
A silent bond that speaks anew.

Through every brush, a story we weave,
In every moment, we choose to believe.
The heart responds to every sign,
In subtle touch, our souls entwine.

Together, we discover the way,
In simple gestures, love will sway.
The art of touch, forever stays,
In quiet whispers, through all our days.

Frameworks of Emotion

In valleys deep where feelings dwell,
We build the frameworks, cast the spell.
With every thought, a structure formed,
In these foundations, hearts are warmed.

Dancing shadows, flickers bright,
In stormy weather, we unite.
With every laugh, joy's frame expands,
In trepidation, we take hands.

Through whispered hopes and soft regrets,
We forge the bonds, we won't forget.
In all our laughter, all our tears,
The frameworks rise throughout the years.

An architecture of love defined,
In every corner, peace aligned.
Through every storm, through every quake,
These frameworks hold, no hearts can break.

So let us build with bricks of trust,
In this foundation, love is a must.
Frameworks strong, forever stand,
In the structure of a held hand.

Distances Measured in Kindness

In whispers soft, we stitch the space,
Where hearts can dance, and dreams embrace.
Each smile a bridge, each touch a thread,
A tapestry of words unsaid.

Through miles apart, we share the glow,
A warmth that only kindness knows.
Distance shrinks, where love expands,
In unseen paths, we hold the hands.

A simple gesture, a gentle nod,
Can lighten burdens under the sod.
Each act of care, a starry guide,
Illuminating paths we stride.

Though shadows stretch, and days grow long,
Together we rise, united and strong.
In kindness found, our hearts entwine,
Across the gaps, your soul is mine.

So let the miles roll far away,
As kindness blooms with each new day.
With every heartbeat, we are near,
Distances fade when hearts are clear.

Intersection of Hearts

At crossroads where our spirits meet,
A silent space, yet bittersweet.
In glances shared, a story spun,
Two paths collide, two lives begun.

With every laugh, a spark ignites,
In shadows long, we chase the lights.
Hearts synchronize, a pulsing beat,
A rhythm found, so warm, so sweet.

In moments fleeting, magic thrives,
Within the intersecting lives.
Hope dances lightly on the air,
In every glance, a whispered prayer.

Beneath the stars, our secrets blend,
A silent pact, where dreams transcend.
With open arms, we take the leap,
In this embrace, our promise deep.

So let the world outside forget,
While we weave dreams without regret.
In intersections, hearts rely,
Two souls unite beneath the sky.

Points of Perspective

From every view, a story told,
In fractured light, the truth unfolds.
Each angle shifts the way we see,
In hues of life, we find the key.

A step aside, and worlds collide,
New lenses formed on the wild ride.
Through varied eyes, we learn to feel,
The heart's own lens, a wondrous reel.

In shadows cast, and colors bright,
We chart the course through wrong and right.
With every shift, we start to see,
The beauty born in diversity.

In moments shared, we bridge the gap,
Each heart a globe, each mind a map.
Points of view become the dance,
In every glance, we take a chance.

To navigate the paths unknown,
With open hearts, we've always grown.
In points connected, we are free,
Together framed in harmony.

Grids of Grace

In every square, a breath of space,
We find the threads, the grids of grace.
Within the lines, our stories weave,
A canvas bright, where we believe.

With every corner, new hopes arise,
In whispered dreams, we touch the skies.
Compassion flows, a healing stream,
In every heart, we plant the dream.

Through highs and lows, the patterns form,
In chaos pure, we find the norm.
Across the grid, we share the load,
In unity, we lift the road.

So let the dance of grace unfold,
In gentle moves, the truth be told.
Within the lines, our spirits trace,
The bonds we share, in grids of grace.

Together forged, we pave the way,
In every heart, a bright array.
With threads of love, we sew the seam,
In grids of grace, we find the dream.

Clusters of Caring

In the garden of hearts, they bloom bright,
Gentle whispers beneath the moonlight.
Soft hands reaching across the divide,
Together we flourish, with love as our guide.

Nurtured by warmth, each bud takes its stand,
Binding our spirits, a delicate band.
Through storms and through trials, we shelter, we grow,
In clusters of caring, our compassion will flow.

Branches entwined in a beautiful dance,
In moments of silence, we take our chance.
To share in the laughter, to mend every tear,
In clusters of caring, we show that we care.

With roots intertwined, we weather the gale,
In the heart of each challenge, we shall not pale.
For love knows no distance, it breaks every chain,
In clusters of caring, there's joy after pain.

So let us unite, let our voices be clear,
In this vibrant garden, we have nothing to fear.
With blossoms of hope, we shall always stand tall,
In clusters of caring, we answer the call.

Knots of Kindness

In every interaction, a thread is spun,
Knots of kindness unite everyone.
A smile shared freely can light up the dusk,
With gestures of love, in humanity we trust.

Tangled together, our paths intertwine,
In the fabric of life, each moment is fine.
From small acts of grace, to the grandest embrace,
Knots of kindness encircle, a warm, safe space.

Across all divisions, our hearts are the same,
A chain forged with care, without reason for shame.
The ties that we nurture can never unwind,
In knots of kindness, we seek and we find.

With threads of compassion, we patch every hole,
In the tapestry woven, we honor each soul.
Through trials and triumphs, we weather the fight,
In knots of kindness, we shine ever bright.

So tie that first knot, let it carry you far,
Remember the warmth of the kindest star.
In every heart's story, may kindness be told,
In knots of kindness, we gather our gold.

Facets of Forgiveness

In the prism of life, many colors reflect,
Facets of forgiveness, we must all accept.
With shadows of hurt that we've carried too long,
In the light of release, we find where we belong.

Each facet reveals both the pain and the grace,
In the journey of healing, we find our true place.
Letting go gently, it's a powerful way,
In facets of forgiveness, we learn to be okay.

The echoes of sorrow may linger and wane,
Yet forgiving the past can free us from pain.
With each gentle step, we reclaim our own worth,
In facets of forgiveness, we find our rebirth.

Reflections of struggle, they guide us anew,
In the mirror of kindness, we see what is true.
With open hearts, we can bridge every gap,
In facets of forgiveness, we take off the cap.

So shine with the light that you carry inside,
Embrace all the facets, let love be your guide.
In the dance of forgiving, may we all share,
In facets of forgiveness, there's beauty to spare.

Spirals of Sharing

In the circles we form, connections entwine,
Spirals of sharing, where love's light will shine.
With each turn we take, a new story unfolds,
In the dance of our spirits, a treasure to hold.

A ripple of kindness, it spreads far and wide,
In spirals of sharing, there's nothing to hide.
We weave our experiences into the thread,
In the richness of giving, our souls we have fed.

For every small act can grow into more,
Creating compassion we can all restore.
In a world that's divided, let sharing create,
In spirals of sharing, we open the gate.

From the depths of our hearts, let our voices arise,
In the warmth of connection, our spirits shall rise.
Together we journey through laughter and tears,
In spirals of sharing, we conquer our fears.

So let us extend both our hands and our hearts,
In the web of our lives, we each play our parts.
With each thread we offer, may our love ever grow,
In spirals of sharing, we form a new glow.

Mirrored Moments

In glassy reflections, we find our way,
Echoes of laughter where shadows play.
Time whispers softly, a gentle embrace,
Moments unfold in this sacred space.

Fleeting yet timeless, each heartbeat a spark,
Memories captured, igniting the dark.
In every glance, a story untold,
Fragments of life in silver and gold.

Mirrored intentions, a dance of the mind,
Searching for answers, the truth we must find.
In these glimpses, reflections align,
Holding the essence of you and of mine.

A tapestry woven of joy and of tears,
Moments like petals, softening fears.
In the fabric of time, we're stitched to the past,
Memories linger, yet they seldom last.

Through mirrored moments, the heart learns to see,
The beauty of now, the grace of what'll be.
In the silence between, we grow and we learn,
Finding the wisdom with each page we turn.

Edges of Ease

In the quiet corners where shadows meet light,
Whispers of comfort, soft as the night.
A gentle caress, like a breeze through the trees,
Where troubles unravel, in edges of ease.

Breath of the earth, in the stillness we sway,
Moments unhurried, just fading away.
In laughter and silence, our spirits entwine,
Finding the solace of hearts intertwine.

Underneath the stars, where the world feels at peace,
Life unfurls gently, in edges of ease.
Embracing the stillness, the quiet we crave,
A sanctuary built on the love that we save.

Through meadows of thought, we wander and roam,
In brushstrokes of joy, we sketch out our home.
With each step in grace, the stars we release,
Carving our path in these edges of ease.

Here in this moment, we breathe in the calm,
Wrapped in the stillness, a soft, loving balm.
Where worries disperse like fog on the breeze,
Together we flourish, in edges of ease.

Cultivated Connections

In gardens of words, we plant our seeds,
Watering thoughts, fulfilling our needs.
Every shared smile, a flower in bloom,
Cultivated connections, dispelling the gloom.

Hands reach together, in warmth and in trust,
Roots intertwining, as all friendships must.
Through seasons of laughter, through trials endured,
Each moment a harvest, our spirits assured.

Nurtured by kindness, we grow strong and free,
Blooming in colors, as vibrant as can be.
In fields of togetherness, laughter takes flight,
Cultivated connections, a radiant light.

With patience and care, we shape our own fate,
In the bonds that we weave, discovering fate.
Everlasting ties, like branches embrace,
Cultivated connections, our shared sacred space.

As seasons may change, our roots will remain,
Bound by the love, through joy and through pain.
Together we flourish, a gift to behold,
Cultivated connections, more precious than gold.

Sculpted Smiles

In the warmth of laughter, our spirits unfold,
Sculpted smiles shining, more precious than gold.
Carved from the moments that brighten our days,
A testament crafted in unspoken ways.

Each curve a reflection of hearts that embrace,
Mapping the journeys we honor with grace.
Through trials and triumphs, our faces composed,
Sculpted smiles whisper the love we have chose.

In the canvas of life, we paint with our light,
Brushing our shadows, revealing the bright.
With each shared glance, we build and inspire,
Sculpted smiles warming the hearts we desire.

In echoes of joy, the world finds its beat,
Crafted connections become our heartbeat.
Through every endeavor, our light we compile,
Sculpted smiles linger, transcending each mile.

With every soft giggle, our spirits ascend,
Sculpted smiles whisper, we're never alone, friend.
In laughter and joy, we learn to embrace,
The beauty of living, an eternal grace.

Flows of Faith

In shadows deep, a light will rise,
A whisper soft, beneath the skies.
With every step, the heart will grow,
In streams of faith, our spirits flow.

The path is steep, yet we will climb,
With hopes that dance, like bells in chime.
Through trials faced, we find our strength,
In love's embrace, we go the length.

When storms may rage, we hold our ground,
Each drop of rain, a sacred sound.
In unity, our voices blend,
A chorus strong, on dreams we depend.

With every tear, a seed we sow,
In nature's grace, our faith will grow.
Thus onward still, our journey's true,
With flows of faith, we'll see it through.

In quiet moments, hear the call,
The strength in faith, it conquers all.
Through valleys low and peaks so high,
We rise as one, beneath the sky.

Canvas of Care

Brush strokes of kindness on life's display,
Each gentle touch, a bright array.
Colors of love in every hue,
A canvas wild, yet warm and true.

With tender hearts, we paint the morn,
In laughter shared, new bonds are born.
Each helping hand, a vibrant mark,
In shades of hope, we light the dark.

Through trials faced, we draw anew,
In every struggle, courage grew.
United strong, our spirits soar,
In this great art, we're never poor.

The strokes of grief may shade the scene,
Yet in the sorrow, love is keen.
With every tear, a story's told,
A canvas bright, in hues of gold.

As time goes on, the masterpiece,
Transforms with age, yet finds its peace.
In strokes of care, we find the way,
To forge a life, where hope will stay.

Breaths of Bravery

In silence deep, we find our voice,
To stand and speak, to make a choice.
With hearts ablaze, we take the leap,
In breaths of bravery, our dreams we keep.

Each step we take, a mountain moved,
Within the fear, our courage proved.
The echoes vast of stories shared,
In breaths of bravery, we are prepared.

When shadows loom, we'll face the night,
With every breath, we seek the light.
Through trials harsh, our spirits rise,
In breaths of bravery, we touch the skies.

For every fall, we find our ground,
In every loss, the strength is found.
Together strong, our voices sing,
In breaths of bravery, new hope we bring.

With every heartbeat, we make our stand,
In unity, we take a hand.
For life is but a fleeting flame,
In breaths of bravery, we stake our claim.

Tiers of Truth

Beneath the layers, wisdom hides,
In every tale, the heart abides.
With open eyes, we seek to learn,
In tiers of truth, our spirits yearn.

The first tier whispers, soft and pure,
A gentle call, a love secure.
Within its grasp, we feel the spark,
In every truth, a journey's arc.

As layers peel, the world appears,
In hues of joy, and tempered fears.
The second tier, a deeper dive,
Where shadows dance, our thoughts arrive.

Through trials faced, we find our way,
In every choice, the price we pay.
The third tier calls, a weighty test,
In honesty, we find our rest.

So let us climb, to heights unknown,
In tiers of truth, our seeds are sown.
With every step, our wisdom grows,
In life's rich layers, the spirit glows.

For truth, my friend, is ever clear,
A guiding light, we hold so dear.
In every heart, a voice of grace,
In tiers of truth, we find our place.

Circles of Comfort

In the warmth of gentle arms,
We find solace, soft and calm,
Round the fire, stories shared,
In these circles, hearts are aired.

Laughter echoes, bright and clear,
Wrapped in joy, we hold each dear,
Moments woven, tight and strong,
Here together, we belong.

Comfort zones, where we reside,
In the light, there's naught to hide,
Through the seasons, hand in hand,
Together we will always stand.

Walls may rise, but love breaks through,
In our hearts, we'll see it true,
Through every trial, we will cope,
In each circle, there is hope.

As the world spins ever fast,
In these moments, we hold fast,
Circles drawn, a sacred space,
In this comfort, we find grace.

Dynamic Expressions

Colors dance upon the page,
Whispers of a vibrant stage,
Every brushstroke tells a tale,
In each hue, emotions sail.

Rhythms pulse in the night air,
Voices rise, a lively flare,
Movement flows like river bright,
Dynamic forms take joyful flight.

Words like waves, they crash and swell,
In their cadence, secrets dwell,
Exclamations, soft and bold,
Stories woven, truth retold.

Each expression, raw and free,
A fleeting glance at what could be,
In the chaos, art unfolds,
Links of spirit, grace molds.

In every corner of the mind,
Dynamic tales we seek to find,
Expressions fluid as the sea,
In art's embrace, we're truly free.

Shadows Beneath the Surface

Beneath the calm, where waters lie,
Lurk the shadows, deep and sly,
Mysteries swirl in twilight's grip,
Secrets hidden, on the tip.

Light may dance upon the tide,
But darkness whispers, seeks to hide,
Echoes linger in twilight's mist,
Stories long forgotten twist.

Glimpses fleeting, truth obscured,
In the silence, hearts are stirred,
Shadows weave their intricate thread,
In the depths, where souls are led.

Every ripple holds a tale,
Of hidden dreams that softly sail,
Beneath the surface, life abounds,
In the quiet, wisdom sounds.

Though the light seems bright and clear,
Embrace the shadows, hold them near,
For in that depth, the heart finds grace,
In those shadows, we find place.

Lines Connecting Stories

In the web of time we tread,
Lines connect what's left unsaid,
Every heart a chapter bold,
In each story, wisdom told.

Paths intertwine, they wend and weave,
In this dance, we learn to believe,
Threads of laughter, threads of tears,
In every stitch, we conquer fears.

Each life a book, each tale a spark,
In the dark, we find our mark,
Lines binding us in shared endeavor,
Together bound, now and forever.

Through the pages, stories flow,
In every heart, a vibrant glow,
Connections forged through joy and pain,
In this symphony, we remain.

So let us write, our tales in ink,
With every line, together think,
Connected stories, rich and grand,
In shared moments, hand in hand.

Angles of Affection

In the twilight where shadows lie,
Hearts converge beneath the sky.
Gentle whispers fill the air,
In every glance, a silent prayer.

Moments captured, time stands still,
Each touch sends a warm goodwill.
Lines of fate drawn near and far,
Love's reflection, a shining star.

Brush of hands in tender grace,
Every heartbeat finds its place.
In angles sharp and curves that blend,
A dance of souls that will not end.

Echoes linger in the night,
Softest sighs hold pure delight.
Promises woven in the dark,
Each vow brighter than a spark.

Together we rise, forever bound,
In silent joy, our truth profound.
Angles shift, but never break,
In love's embrace, our hearts awake.

Curves of Connection

In the gentle sway of leaves,
Nature speaks, and the heart believes.
Curves that intertwine with grace,
A warm smile, a familiar face.

Through winding paths our spirits flow,
In every turn, new seeds we sow.
The laughter shared, a bridge we span,
Hands entwined, we dream and plan.

As rivers turn in endless flight,
So do we, through day and night.
Soft silhouettes in the fading light,
Together fierce, together bright.

In moments silent, truths unfold,
Stories shared, forever told.
Curves of joy, this we've known,
In every heartbeat, love has grown.

With every bend, our spirits rise,
Catching stars within our eyes.
In cosmic dance, we find our name,
Two souls ignited, one burning flame.

Lines of Lost Intent

In ink-stained pages, tales of old,
Lost intentions, dreams untold.
Words can falter, voices fade,
In silent nights, the heart is swayed.

Echoes linger of what we sought,
In shadows cast by battles fought.
Lines once drawn now blurred and thin,
The ghost of passion beckons in.

Faded letters, the touch of ink,
In every pause, we stop and think.
Promises crushed beneath the weight,
The heavy hand of twisted fate.

Yet within the cracks, hope may bloom,
Lost intent, but love finds room.
For every tear, a lesson learned,
In ashes, still, the fire burned.

So let us write what's yet to be,
New lines etched in memory.
For in the depth of every fall,
A chance to rise and stand up tall.

Shapes of Silent Understanding

In quiet corners where thoughts align,
Shapes emerge, a design so fine.
Unspoken words, a knowing glance,
Two hearts entwined, a timeless dance.

In curves of thought, we find our way,
Through swirling moments of night and day.
Every breath a conversation shared,
In the spaces where silence cared.

Gentle nods, a soft embrace,
Carving out our sacred space.
Here in shadows, love takes flight,
Painting dreams with soft moonlight.

With whispers low, our spirits rise,
In this realm, the truth belies.
Shapes of joy, so gently drawn,
In twilight's glow, a new dawn.

This understanding, sweet and rare,
In every heartbeat, love laid bare.
Shapes of silent warmth, we find,
Two souls forever intertwined.

Touchpoints of Truth

In silence we find our way,
Each whisper holds a key.
The shadows dance in light of day,
Revealing what must be.

Through eyes that seek, the heart can see,
A world both vast and small.
Connections form like roots of trees,
A truth that binds us all.

In moments shared, the fabric weaves,
Threads of joy and pain.
Each memory a leaf that cleaves,
To branches strong, unchained.

With every step, our paths align,
In trust, we stand as one.
The fates entwine like hills that twine,
Beneath the rising sun.

So linger here in quiet thought,
Embrace the sacred space.
For touchpoints stitched with love are wrought,
To guide us through this race.

The Balance of Being

In stillness lies the secret truth,
A dance of shadow and light.
To balance chaos and sweet youth,
We navigate the night.

Each heartbeat sings a timeless song,
A rhythm deep and strong.
In harmony where we belong,
The world hums along.

With open arms to hold the weight,
Of joy and sorrow's flow.
Embrace the tides of love and fate,
To learn and ever grow.

In nature's arms, we find our ground,
The earth beneath our feet.
Awake in beauty, soft and sound,
Life's balance, pure and sweet.

So breathe the air, let calmness reign,
Within the depths of being.
For in the struggle, there's no pain,
Just pure and vibrant seeing.

Unfolding the Heart's Canvas

With gentle strokes, we paint our dreams,
On canvas stretched so wide.
Each color bursts and softly gleams,
Revealing what's inside.

In layers formed from hopes and fears,
The brush of life glides on.
With every touch, we draft the years,
Until the dark is gone.

The heart expands with every hue,
In patterns rich and bold.
Each splash of love, a vibrant view,
A story yet untold.

Embrace the chaos, blend the shades,
For art is always free.
In every mark, a spark invades,
Connecting you and me.

So let your spirit rise and soar,
As colors blend and part.
In every stroke, we find the core,
The beauty of the heart.

Veins of Vulnerability

In honesty, the truth runs deep,
Like rivers feeding roots.
We dare to share what wounds we keep,
And wear our fragile suits.

Behind the mask, the heart beats loud,
In whispers soft and clear.
To break the silence of the crowd,
Is to defy the fear.

Each scar a tale of battles won,
Of trials faced with grace.
In openness, we find the sun,
And carve a sacred space.

With every crest and trough we chart,
The bonds of trust entwine.
Through storms, we learn the strength of heart,
In hopes that brightly shine.

So let us cherish all we share,
The beauty found in scars.
For in our veins, together bare,
We radiate like stars.

Milton Keynes UK
Ingram Content Group UK Ltd.
UKHW022049111124
451035UK00014B/1011

9 789916 866276